WHEN DADDY TUCKS THE STARS IN

By: Erik Usher

This book is dedicated to all the families of those First responders who selflessly spend nights away from their families to help yours.

More importantly, this is for my wonderful wife who had to answer this questions to our two children Maya and Max!

"When Daddy Tucks The Stars In"
Copyright © 2024 by Erik Usher

All rights reserved. No part of this publication may be reproduced or transmitted in any form or by any means, electronic or mechanical, Including photocopying, recording or any information storage and retrieval system, without written permission from the copyright owner.

"Why isn't Daddy home tonight?" asked Max, hugging his stuffed dalmatian tightly. The soft glow of his bedside lamp lit up the room as he gazed at Mommy with curious eyes.

"Well, Max," said Mom, tucking him in, "Daddy is out helping people tonight. He's a firefighter, and that means he's always ready to protect people when they're in trouble."

"Is Daddy putting out big fires?" Max asked, his eyes wide with wonder.

"Sometimes," Mom said with a nod. "But he also helps in so many other ways, like rescuing people or making sure their homes are safe."

"Is it scary for him?" Max whispered.

"A little," Mom said softly. "But Daddy is very brave. He trains with his team to stay safe and to protect others, no matter how hard the job is."

"Does Daddy think about me when he's at work?" Max asked.

"Always," said Mom. "He says you're his little spark of courage. Thinking of you makes him brave, even on the toughest nights."

"But why does he have to work at night?"

"Because emergencies can happen anytime," Mom explained. "And Daddy wants to make sure people have someone to help them when they need it most."

"Will he come home soon?" Max asked as he yawned.

"Yes, sweetheart," Mom said, pulling the blanket snug around him. "And when he does, he'll be so happy to see you. He loves hearing about your dreams."

That night, Max dreamed of his dad driving his firetruck under the stars, helping people stay safe. Even though he wasn't home, he knew he was a hero, and the stars were watching over both of them.

Pictures of my Dad

Pictures of me and my Dad

Drawings of my Dad

My favorite things about my Dad

Drawings of my Dad at work

Drawings of Mom and Dad

Drawings of Mom tucking me in

My favorite things about my Mom

www.ingramcontent.com/pod-product-compliance
Lightning Source LLC
Chambersburg PA
CBRC090840010526
44119CB00045B/501